BLESS THIS
HOME

BLESS THIS HOME

William R. Nirote

THE PILGRIM PRESS
CLEVELAND

For Arevena Nirote

who made our house a home

The Pilgrim Press, 700 Prospect Avenue, Cleveland, Ohio 44115
thepilgrimpress.com
© 2014 by William R. Nirote

Printed in the United States of America on acid-free paper

17   16   15   14   13   5   4   3   2   1

CONTENTS

꧁꧂

꧁꧂

INTRODUCTION

Two of the markers of the people of God throughout the Scriptures are hospitality and blessing. *Bless This Home* is a service of hospitality to bless one's dwelling and its residents.

The minister leading this blessing of a home is encouraged to make this a celebration. It would be helpful for the minister to meet with the resident(s) before the service to determine what parts of *Bless This Home* are relevant for this blessing. The minister ought to encourage the resident(s) to invite family, friends and neighbors for this ritual. This ritual of *Bless This Home* is meant to be a celebration, a declaration of a household's faith and to ask God for divine favor.

The Christian Scriptures remind us of how followers of the Way gathered and shared what was held in common among them. They gathered devoting themselves to Apostles' teachings, breaking of bread, prayers and singing. Many of these gatherings were in homes where believers, seekers and new converts were all welcomed. These homes were a place of security and peace. These homes were a place where old teachings and new visions were shared and missions were launched.

With roots in the Hebrew tradition, Christianity continued the tradition of blessing, or choosing life over death, blessing over curse, love over hate. Asking for divine favor and seeking the way of God was to choose life, blessing and love.

In this document, the title "Minister" was chosen because of the various kinds of ordained and non-ordained leadership diversity found within various settings. The term "Minister" is meant to be inclusive for these various kinds of church leadership.

The symbol "+" is meant to prompt the Minister to make the sign of the cross. The sign of the cross is a symbol of both forgiveness and God's blessing. The Minister making the sign of the cross is also reminding all assembled of our baptisms, our entrance into the Church Universal and the participation of all in the royal priesthood of all believers.

A candle may be used in *Bless This Home* as a symbol of God's presence. An individual may be designated before the blessing of a home to light the candle at the appropriate time.

In the ever increasing demands on church leaders, *Bless This Home* is meant to be a worship resource guiding the Minister and the resident(s) of a home through a blessing. May God bless you, the Minister, in your calling and faithful service to God.

———◆———

A word of thanks to Janice Brown, Kim Martin Sadler, Aimée Jannsohn, and others at The Pilgrim Press for their guidance in this resource's publication. Special thanks must be given to Thomas E. Dipko, who offered resources, wisdom, encouragement and refinement to the process of writing and editing *Bless This Home*.

GATHERING

I

GATHERING

If conditions allow, the gathering is outside the entrance to the home. With the challenges of new construction or weather conditions, the gathering may need to be held inside in a foyer or some other accessible room. These words may be said by the resident's Minister with the people gathered.

Words of Gathering

MINISTER: The Lord be with you.

PEOPLE: And also with you.

MINISTER: We gather in the name of God our Creator, our Redeemer, and our Comforter.

PEOPLE: Amen.

Prayers of Gathering

MINISTER: Let us pray.
Holy One, we gather to ask your blessing
on this (apartment, condominium, house)
and for the people who will reside in these walls.
As we gather (inside from the elements, outside in
    the elements),
we thank you for how this structure
will protect (this one, this family, these families,
    these people)
from the heat of summer,
from the cold of winter,
from the harsh winds,
from the scorching sun
and from the storms of moisture (rain, hail, sleet
    and snow).
We pray this (apartment, condominium, house)
will be protected by your gracious hand,
as those inside will be protected by this home.
Amen.

MINISTER: The Psalmist reminds us:
"Unless the Lord builds the house,
those who build it labor in vain." Psalm 127:1.

In the Hebrew Scriptures
we learn that the household of Joshua
turned from the false gods of this world
and chose to follow God, saying,
"As for me and my household,
we will serve the Lord." Joshua 24:15c.

This household has chosen to follow God,
in the example of Jesus Christ,
as empowered by the Holy Spirit.
This household has chosen to ask God's blessing
    upon this house,
setting it aside for holy use,
modeling the love and care of Christ,
practicing hospitality as modeled in the church.

Therefore, this blessing,
will be done in an act of boldness and faith,
declaring not only God's welcome
but God's presence in these walls.

THE BLESSING

2

꧁

THE BLESSING

꧂

Words of Explanation

Addressing the resident(s).

MINISTER: In Genesis we learn that God is the
    Creator of all
and we are part of God's good creation.
You may consider this (apartment, condominium,
    house) to be your own.
At best, you are (stewards, a steward) of this
    (apartment, condominium, house)
until those who come after you
will one day reside in this place.
You are a steward,

creating an environment that is
faithful, supportive, creative and loving
in this place.
A place where God's presence is acknowledged
and welcomed.

Addressing all gathered if there is one resident.

MINISTER: Asking God's blessing on (an apartment,
a condominium, a house)
and the one who resides here,
declares this person's faith commitment.

Addressing all gathered if there is more than one resident.

MINISTER: Asking God's blessing on (an apartment,
a condominium, a house) and household
is setting a foundation.
On this foundation
the Apostle Paul said we are to,
"Be subject to one another out of reverence
for Christ." Ephesians 5:21.
This home shares in the joy of a community
as part of God's good creation.

The Blessing

MINISTER: Loving God,
on this day we ask your blessing
upon this (apartment, condominium, house)
    and its resident(s).
May this home be a safe harbor
from the world's treacherous waters.
May this home be a place of rest and relaxation.
May this home be a place of exercise and
    rejuvenation.
May this home be a place of giving and forgiving.
May this home be a place where people can sing
the songs of life and of eternal life.
May this home be a blessing for others who visit,
sensing your loving presence.
May this home be filled with your love
and the love of (those, the one) who inhabit(s)
    this home.
This blessing we pray
in the name of the Eternal God,
who was, and is and shall always be. (+) Amen.

PEOPLE: May the blessing of God be here!

Lighting of a candle near the entrance.

MINISTER: We now light this candle,
a symbol of God's presence in this place.
As the flame warms this home,
may this place be a home of laughter and love,
a place of rest, restoration and reconciliation.

3

✿

BLESSINGS FOR INDIVIDUAL
ROOMS OF THE HOME

✿

Then the righteous will answer him, "Lord, when was it that we saw you hungry and gave you food, or thirsty and gave you something to drink? And when was it that we saw you a stranger and welcomed you, or naked and gave you clothing? And when was it that we saw you sick or in prison and visited you?" And the king will answer them, "Truly I tell you, just as you did it to one of the least of these who are members of my family, you did it to me." Matthew 25:37–40.

The following individual blessings may be said where appropriate.

✿ **19** ✿

FOYER

MINISTER: Welcoming God,
we ask your blessing on this foyer,
the entrance into this home.
May all who come to this home be welcomed,
as Christ Jesus among us.
May family and friends sense the blessing
of arriving in this place.

PEOPLE: May the blessing of God be here!

LIVING ROOM

MINISTER: Accepting God,
we ask your blessing on this living room,
a place of receiving others.
May others sense your loving presence in this room,
where guests are received
and where words are spoken.
May all who are received here
sense your blessing on this household.

PEOPLE: May the blessing of God be here!

> *"The grace of the Lord Jesus Christ, the love of God,
> and the communion of the Holy Spirit be with all of
> you."* II Corinthians 13:13

KITCHEN

MINISTER: Abundant God,
we thank you and ask for your blessing
on the hands that will prepare the meals of this home.
We thank you for the hands in our food chain,
those that planted crops and raised animals,
harvested and shipped,
and hands that brought food to market.
May all who benefit from this kitchen
sense the blessing of the abundance of your creation
and our need to share among ourselves
and with those who are hungry.

PEOPLE: May the blessing of God be here!

Jesus said to them, "I am the bread of life.
Whoever comes to me will never be hungry, and
whoever believes in me will never be thirsty."
John 6:35

DINING ROOM

MINISTER: Nurturing God,
may your blessing be upon those
who will gather in this room
to share meals and conversation.
May those who gather
be nourished in body and in spirit.

PEOPLE: May the blessing of God be here!

*"Blessed are those who hunger and thirst for
righteousness, for they will be filled."* Matthew 5:6

Family Room

MINISTER: Living God,
in this place of gathering family and friends
for entertainment and conversation,
homework and games,
nourish the people who will gather in this place.
May all who gather in this room
sense the light, life and love of the Christ among us.
Amen.

PEOPLE: May the blessing of God be here!

> *"How precious is your steadfast love, O God!*
> *All people may take refuge in the shadow of your wings.*
> *They feast on the abundance of your house,*
> *and you give them drink from the river of your delights.*
> *For with you is the fountain of life;*
> *in your light we see light." Psalm 36:7–9*

CHILD'S/CHILDREN'S BEDROOM(S)

[Jesus] said to them, "Let the little children come to me; do not stop them; for it is to such as these that the [dominion] of God belongs. Truly I tell you, whoever does not receive the [dominion] of God as a little child will never enter it." And [Jesus] took them up in his arms, laid his hands on them, and blessed them. Mark 10:14b–16

MINISTER: Blessing God,
as Jesus blessed little children,
may your blessing be upon the child (children)
who will rest in (this/these) room(s)
and ready themselves for daily journeys.
May the child (children) be kept from all harm,
as (she/he/they) grow(s) in stature, knowledge
    and wisdom.

PEOPLE: May the blessing of God be here!

MASTER BEDROOM *(for a single person)*

MINISTER: Loving God,
my your blessing be upon this room
where there may be rest and
a place for making one ready for daily journeys.
May this be a sacred space and at times,
a place of blessed solitude from the noise of this world.

PEOPLE: May the blessing of God be here!

MASTER BEDROOM *(for a couple)*

MINISTER: Loving God,
may your blessing be upon this room
where there may rest, and shared joy
in the comfort and blessing of a partner's presence,
in the privacy of intimate discussions and
a place for making one ready for daily journeys.
May this be a sacred space for partners and at times,
a place of blessed solitude from the noise of this world.

PEOPLE: May the blessing of God be here!

> *"So then you are no longer strangers and aliens,*
> *but you are citizens with the saints and also members*
> *of the household of God, built upon the foundation of*
> *the apostles and prophets, with Christ Jesus himself as*
> *the cornerstone. In him the whole structure is joined*
> *together and grows into a holy temple in the Lord; in*
> *whom you also are built together spiritually into a*
> *dwelling place for God."* Ephesians 2:19–22

STUDY/DEN

MINISTER: Redeeming God,
You are our constant,
in times of prosperity and times of trouble,
in times of instruction and times of mundane duties,
in times of discovery and times of thanksgiving,
you are ever with us and for us.
May your blessing be upon this room,
where knowledge and wisdom are sought,
where reflection and focus may be found,
and where hope and compassion may be practiced.

PEOPLE: May the blessing of God be here!

> *"Your word is a lamp to my feet and a light to my path."*
> Psalm 119:105

BATHROOM(S)

MINISTER: Righteous God,
while we cannot ever be fully righteous
    by what we have done,
Christ has made us clean in your sight.
In this room may (this one, this family, these families,
    these people)
perform daily tasks of hygiene
that will provide good health.
May this space bless (this one, this family,
    these families, these people)
with good health and preservation of life.

PEOPLE: May the blessing of God be here!

*"But when you fast, put oil on your head and
wash your face."* Matthew 6:17

Work Room

Minister: In this work room
where laundry is cleaned, folded, pressed or hung,
bless the hands that provide this service
    to this household.
May this space bless (the one, this family,
    these families, these people)
with clothing and towels, and various items
    for cleaning.
May this space bless (the one, this family,
    these families, these people)
with the ability to clean and care for this home.

People: May the blessing of God be here!

Storage Room

MINISTER: In this place of storage of keepsakes,
holiday decorations and other items,
may the resident(s) recognize
these things will one day rust or rot,
be destroyed or stolen.
May this space be a reminder
to seek God's dominion
where neither moth, nor rust can destroy,
where thieves cannot break in and steal.

PEOPLE: May the blessing of God be here!

> *"Do not store up for yourselves treasures on earth,*
> *where moth and rust consume and where thieves break*
> *in and steal; but store up for yourselves treasures in*
> *heaven, where neither moth nor rust consumes and*
> *where thieves do not break in and steal. For where*
> *your treasure is, there your heart will be also."*
> Matthew 6:19–21

GARAGE

MINISTER: In this place of storage
for transportation, lawn care products,
tools and various other items,
we pray for safety
while in storage and when in use.
May this space bring a welcome to the resident(s)
    coming home
and store the tools to help maintain this home.

PEOPLE: May the blessing of God be here!

> *"O give thanks to [God], for [God] is good;*
> *for [God's] steadfast love endures forever.*
> *Let the redeemed of [God] say so,*
> *those [God] redeemed from trouble*
> *and gathered in from the lands,*
> *from the east and from the west,*
> *from the north and from the south."* Psalm 107:1–3

UTILITY ROOM

MINISTER: In this place where water, electricity,
fuel and lines of communication come into this home,
we pray for safety with these various services.
May these various utility services
bring comfort, hygiene, light, life,
communication and entertainment
to the resident(s) of this home.

PEOPLE: May the blessing of God be here!

Pool/Hot Tub/Exercise Room/Backyard/Garden

MINISTER: In (this place/these places) of recreation
and relaxation,
may there be safety and pleasure,
exercise and good health.

PEOPLE: May the blessing of God be here!

CLOSING

4

CLOSING

MINISTER: A home is a place
where we retreat from daily challenges
in a place where we can once again
ready ourselves for another day's work.
A home is a place where relationships are built,
lessons of God and God's good creation are shared,
and we are lovingly challenged
to be all that God has created us to be.

We have asked God's blessing on this home
and (the one, the ones) who reside(s) here.
Now, let us rejoice in God's presence in this place
and with (the one, the ones) who reside(s) here.
May we celebrate that God is indeed in this place.

Let us pray.
Holy One,
Hear the requests of your servants
for your blessing to be upon this home
and its resident(s).
May the inhabitant(s) of this home
find peace in this place.
May (his, her, their) commitment to you
and to the care of all your creation
be evident in (his, her, their) stewardship
of this residence,
and to all who live or visit in this place.

May the love witnessed in this home
be an example for all.
These things we pray,
God our Creator,
(+) Christ our Redeemer,
Holy Spirit our Comforter.
Amen.